T0244974

FIND ME WHEN
YOU'RE READY

FIND ME WHEN YOU'RE READY

POEMS

PERRY JANES

Curbstone Books / Northwestern University Press
Evanston, Illinois

Curbstone Books
Northwestern University Press
www.nupress.northwestern.edu

Copyright © 2024 by Northwestern University. Published 2024 by
Curbstone Books / Northwestern University Press. All rights reserved.

Printed in the United States of America

10 9 8 7 6 5 4 3 2 1

Library of Congress Cataloging-in-Publication Data

Names: Janes, Perry, author.
Title: Find me when you're ready : poems / Perry Janes.
Description: Evanston : Curbstone Books/Northwestern University Press, 2024.
Identifiers: LCCN 2024013000 | ISBN 9780810147645 (paperback) | ISBN
    9780810147652 (ebook)
Subjects: LCGFT: Poetry.
Classification: LCC PS3610.A56828 F56 2024 | DDC 811/.6—dc23/
    eng/20240321
LC record available at https://lccn.loc.gov/2024013000

For my parents, with love

CONTENTS

ACT THREE

ACT FOUR

ACT FIVE

FIND ME WHEN YOU'RE READY

BACKSTORY

The sounds of cars labored past
the windows of my childhood home
located within concentric rings of road
spun out from Detroit's city center.
On 12 Mile, each engine's rumbling
presence was punctuated hourly
by trains troubling the viaduct beneath
which traffic signals switched colors

patiently. In this way, I came to love
the sounds of large things hurtling past,
each car or truck only occasionally
turning late into our driveway, high beams
reaching past slat blinds where we, wrapped
in our anticipation, peered out, watching
as the shape of some backlit vehicle
reversed into the road without stopping
for us on that particular night.

LOVE POEM AS TROJAN HORSE

The forest fires above Los Angeles have crept down
the hills overnight, where this morning their scorched
sunrise rouges my fiddlehead fern. Sometimes
hope is a question of redirecting the camera.

A friend tells me he has to trick himself into feeling
anything but numb for the world. What won't burn?
Not the patchwork quilt Tina bought
for our engagement. Not the brewery growlers

stacked along our wine crate bookshelves, teacups
glazed with our fingerprints. The fake stars
glued to our ceiling in constellations forever
spelling fortune. Not the anything we truly cherish—

I used to prize clarity without compromise.
I used to want suffering center-stage, well lit
in the lens. Now, it's changed. So many
routes in the heart's city, steadily walled.

So much need for a gentle hand pulling
focus from one fire to another, the tug
that leads me from my window out
into the night, our night, a blanket

tossed around our shoulders, full
bellies swaying, her body stamped
on mine as we stumble to the gates.
If it must be ruin, if it must come

to ruin: Love, open me.

ACT ONE

Why is childhood—oh, tinfoil treasures,

oh, the rustling of lead, lovely and foreboding—
our only origin, our only longing?
Why is manhood, which takes the place of ripeness,
an endless highway,
Sahara yellow?

—Adam Zagajewski, "Tierra del Fuego" (trans. Clare Cavanagh)

HOME REMEDY

You light the match and feel it
        squirm, the blunt-head tick buried
behind your knee. You think
        nothing has ever felt so

intimate, nub mouth carving its own
        entry. Even entertain the idea of
keeping it: little ride-along, little hunger.
        Why turn away what claims you

as desirable? You bare your ankles
        for what bites in the brush.
You count the seconds it takes
        for them to burn—what was it

your mother said, once? *Pretend
        fearlessness?* There will always be
ways the small and unwanted survive:
        feasts of dead

skin and hair follicles, wounds
        holy with eggs, and though
it repulses you, that mouth
        burrowed below your skin,

hind legs kicking with effort
        or pleasure, you see yourself
in the gesture: lips smashed
        to what hardly knows you're there,

what feeds you almost in spite
        of itself.

ODE TO HYDRANGEAS ENDING IN
REFLECTION ON A CHILDHOOD VISIT FROM
THE EMERGENCY HOME NURSE; OR, UPON
LEARNING THAT CERTAIN FLOWERS FEED ON
FERTILIZER MADE FROM HUMAN REMAINS

Orchids in the biodome.
        Scorched tires on the street.

I'm walking between sewer grate
        cloches rilled with steam

in a friend's back alley
        on Detroit's east side. It's night.

I describe the land so you understand
        when I write *I pause and say "What a moon"*

to the speedboat in the lawn, the windows
        graffitied God God God you know

I'm not bullshitting. There's a speedboat
        in the lawn. There are *Gods* written

on the houses. It's all one violent collage,
        even flowers mobbing

the fence line—hydrangeas, I think—
        and the neighbor who

I'm told rises each Sunday
        to pour crematorium ash

from John and Jane Does into nail-drawn
        furrows. Their off-colored petals.

Her prayer. I hadn't known
        it worked like this: roots responding to acid

in the loam, blossoms bursting pink
        and blue and red. Would you believe

I raced through youth
        without once digging knuckle-deep

in soil? I hold little
        warmth for what dirties my knees.

So it surprises me when I stoop
        to the ground, cup a nearby bloom, pick

a dead fly's wing from its anther,
        lean close and—

The last thing I want
        is to pluck the flowered head

I had nothing to do with planting or caring for,
        never watered from the garden hose

or shook awake on a cold school morning
        with a thermos of cocoa already steaming,

that I never, not once, noticed
        as it walked down the street

with headphones rattling
        at their poorly glued seams

a bass line pronouncing *i am here*
        i am here i am

here i am here i am
        here.

That I only now know to admire.
          Just one petal. That's all

I take. And like the wafer I never ate
          at school Mass, all that business of *the body*

not really *the body*, I place it
          on my tongue and chew—

It isn't the taste that gets me
          but the color, that sudden red

leaking from my lips, red that calls
          back knuckle and gravel, skinned palms

on bathroom tile, my boyhood
          skull split behind the ear.

Is there anything more tender
          than being a child

bent at the enamel basin?
          Knees to the floor,

pruned to the nape,
          some man picking

dirt from your blood?

THIS MUSIC

As a child, I had a tendency toward the chronic.
Ear infections. Outbursts. Nightmares.
Through five long years, I carouseled
in and out of exam rooms, schoolyards. Through
two more, I curled at the foot of my wire-frame
bed, closest to the open door and its offering
of light. When my mother or father happened
past to find me there, late or not-so-late—
they would stop to sing me lullabies,
wordless ditties I now know they must have
forgotten the lyrics for. Eventually I'd fall
asleep, and when I woke hours later to find
blood on my pillow, urine-wet sheets,
the ritual recommenced. I never wondered
what these intrusions meant for their own
sleepless nights, if they whistled the same melody
through twelve-hour days and graveyard shifts,
into grocery bags knotted with discount produce
or phones left off the cradle to reject angry
collectors, if they ever tired of it, each evening
ending with their hands cupped at my ears
where they hummed their off-key tune
to soothe me back to sleep. Years later,
in high school, the gaunt-faced teacher
already eyeing college admissions assigned us
to write about *a period of suffering or struggle
in our lives*. When I stood at the front
of the class to recite what I'd written,
even my teacher betrayed his surprise—
and something like satisfaction—
by my little efforts at lyric. *Finally*,
I thought, *some use for it all*, and rushed
home to perform for my parents, pleased
at this music I believed I had made.

NO MATTER HOW MANY TIMES I PASS

the Dollar General parking lot where

concrete bergs sprout improbable

red flowers, the sinkhole photo shoot,

a bride's train graying in coal ash, or

the corner café, mounds of cro-nut sugar

shared between strangers in February sun

—those ruins, again. That word, *ruin*,

some dust storm clouding the scene.

If it's true we learn by imitation,

somewhere, a boy empties himself

on the sidewalk. He understands

how we build only what we can stand to

Little League base runners racing between

dandelion and king devil, knee socks like

rounds of small fire in the shade,

the thousand-and-one tin cans outside

spilled on the curb, sticky,

where a child's shoe ripped from its sole

again, leaving a pile of rubber and canvas,

the panorama sliding out and out—

is this the story I've come to tell?

Of every reason to praise

the shapes we make for loneliness,

praise as a curtain from sorrow

hold, and leave behind. How a man
of sweat and dirt-knuckle devotion
might say *I made this for you* and
leave the gift to crumble in the rain.
Little stone. Little dirt. The truth is
I can play in all the brick and mortar I like.
I will always be half-spent signal,
ruptured pixel obscured by sun.
Maybe that's a blessing. God
of cardboard and bedazzle beads,
electric tape and half-melted crayons
can you see it? This city, silent,
where I wander, waving *hello* to
windows thrown wide (by who?)

may be the most enduring form.
Strange how, sometimes, the narrative
vanishes to be replaced by landscape:
the pipe wrench wind chime,
a white T rag still spotted with blood.
Because I allow myself to ribbon in the light
fallen on the couch, I fade into scenery.
Stupid boy. Stupid city stalled in place.
You should have seen the things I made
from Grandmama's crochet kit:
a toothpick diorama, sawdust snow, streets
with my name on every sign;
some dollhouse figure in the shade,
hingeless doors on every corner

calling me inside.

INSECT LIFE OF MICHIGAN

—*after Lynda Hull*

In those days, I thought the dried-husk
        chrysalis that clung to our cars
                was a type of thumbprint wilderness

pressed on the city. Mornings, fish flies
        rose from Lake St. Clair to paper
                buildings with their ash-

figured swarm. All that spring, my father
        hunched to peel them from the wind-
                shield with a sticky displeasure

I woke to, their cracking pops—chill
        rain tapping the rooftop. Even then, I knew
                there was comfort in this ritual:

the separation of animal hunger
        from its perch. In those days
                my father drove door-to-door

with glossy brochures for log cabin
        A-frames papering the seats
                which is just another way of saying

we were constantly aware,
        my father and I, of where
                we could not be: Alaska,

adulthood, each day that March
        like another word in childhood's
                run-on sentence of undefined

desires, the township names
        my father rolled against his palate—
                Yakutat, Talkeetna, Nikiski—

blurred into a low-note hum
        of engine cough and insects
                caught in the fuel pipe.

Even then I knew
        he would not make a sale.
                Those nights, idling

near the razor weed lakeshore,
        we sat beneath sodium vapor
                streetlamps hovelled

in their own breathing
        shell, a finery
                of wings that trembled

against our labored breath
        while we watched
                the frail chassis peel

from themselves,
        mutely, as though
                without complaint.

SHOOTER

There are things I don't know,
can't know, and maybe don't want to,
including what a man's teeth look like
through a rifle's magnifying scope. Tonight
a frightened anchor on the radio reports
a gunman stalking Interstate 96 firing
into back seats, windshields, drivers behaving
erratically, causing pile-ups. I'm sick of
God and his potholes, the many mouths
opening relentlessly, beneath. Tonight
a costumed boy with ketchup-
colored wounds pressed in his gut
will ring my doorbell with hands held out
expecting something sweet. The truth?
All I want is to sit on the living room
couch with my mother, my father, and not
imagine them as ghosts. To hold
the teacup handle of my partner's wrist
and not to feel for fractures. O eye
on the highway, muzzled median, bullet
meant for my seat: I too have sought
to slow the snaking blur that passes
every afternoon. To cradle something
cold against my chest and feel the judder
as it kicks from my grasp, away.
When I think of you, I imagine just
barely escaping. Your index finger leads
my car's bald tires. Maybe this is love:
not pulling the trigger. Maybe no one
will ever know me so completely. Tonight
all I have is enough to feel grateful for.

My parents in their bodies, my lover in hers.
A parade of costumed children bravely
trying on their deaths. The boy
at my door smiling, those teeth—

PALINODE

You've heard me praise *the blossoms*
bursting pink and blue and red.
The fact of them: dull pastels scraped
by rain. Accuracy is rarely flattering.
Most nights, the stars become a spattering
of semen. Black leather. Halo-
stained creases. Most nights, the couch
looks just like a night sky. When I say "I want
to sink into it" I do not mean float.
When I say it will be the dim rictus of a friend's
smile that betrays you, I mean beware those
who would position themselves backlit above,
hand resting on your shoulder for the photo
still held in its frame. Were you always the same
height? Did his teeth always flash
like that? Like this, you will forget
his voice turning first one, then another
against you. If there is a burning
in the landscape, shield your eyes
against the glare. Light striking
the iris creates a sunset where
no sunset exists. It is so often
what shines, lies.

THE PROBLEM WITH METAMORPHOSIS

—after Fatimah Asghar

You're meat until you're metal. You're Manga until you're Marvel. You're long hair, blond, Virgo bitch avenger with the power of the moon until you're green, bald, a gathering of energy between your fists, feet stuck to your own planet. You know the right words to shout for all your friends to gather at your shoulders, your sidekicks and accomplices, until you don't, until the words are written in code, *power of the sky possess me* or *by the hoary hosts of hogoth!* You're healthy until it's hereditary. Your father was a winged man. He flew too close to orbit. Your father was a weighted chest. He sank into the waves. Wait. You can't remember. You're one shape until you're many. Until you try on every coat from the rack. A gathering of feathers. A fall of rain. A curtain blocking out the sun. A silence until *BOOM!* Sound bubbles, everywhere. You're a hero until you're tired. You're a villain until you win. You're a child, and some days it seems that's all you'll ever be. You're naked, you're not. You're caught beneath a boot heel, pressed against the floor, made to pose, to play, the buttons between your teeth, the thread against your tongue, until—you can fly. You can flame. You can spit lightning and kick up twisters with your heels. It matters what you become until it doesn't anymore. Until all that matters is the change. You're drawn inside a frame until you're projected on a screen. Held inside a pocket. Warmed close to another child's face beneath the covers. "You can be anything," you say. It's a lie, until it isn't.

KILLER OF SHEEP

—*for my friends, after the film of the same
title by Charles Burnett, 1978*

At night, my father leans above his draftsman's desk
to sketch the car, its wheels, the trunk not yet
filled with floaties or baseballs, and when
my mother rises, when she calls him back
to bed, when she slides her hands down

the down against his nape, her fingers
catch, briefly, in the teeth of small gears
clicking behind his nod. Or not. I'm told
some nights what we do becomes who we are.
If I had the choice to make myself

machine, to spit diesel between my teeth,
or to make myself desired, touched
not like a panel with buttons and switches
but something entirely without utility,
pleasurable just to hold, which would I choose?

In the movie, my favorite movie, the mother
shimmies in her nightdress to hold her husband
close, his children running rings around his knees,
each struggling to contain what they understand
will leave before it leaves; the man

leaving anyway, knowing a dozen sheep wait
on the slaughterhouse floor for the iron
tongue that slithers from his palm to drop them
one by one by one by one and I can't help
asking: How long does a man like that keep

any sense of proportion? In the movie
or my kitchen, I can't remember which,
someone's father, I can't remember whose, leaves
and says *find me when you're ready.* I imagine him
out there dropping clues for them (for me?)

to follow. I imagine he isn't very good at it.
Pared fingernails glittering beneath a stoplight,
smashed coffee cups leaking on the corner.
Clue derived from the ancient Greek *clew*
meaning the ball of yarn some idiot

hero unspools as he enters the winding maze
to retrace his steps, to escape. It's all
such serious business, isn't it? This searching
for one another? A man blows a kiss
and snaps the deadbolt closed behind him.

A woman scours the streets for any trace
of movement. A boy unpacks
his father's tools to practice lines,
his sketches and schematics, the swoop
of charcoal etched on vellum, a man's

broad shoulders coming into view.

ACT TWO

tune up
and if you like

drill imagination right through necessity

—A. R. Ammons, "Play"

CREATION MYTH

i

I wanted to be kissed not bitten
when the dare got to me, even if all I knew
of pleasure could be reduced to the Easter eggs
my grandmother dyed, hollow shells I liked to feed
to the garbage disposal, even if seven
was old enough to know not to play the older
boy's game, not to set foot inside that room, empty
except for construction paper children, headless
crayons, plush tigers, cockeyed, all of it
trying so hard to appear innocuous.

ii

And so there is before and after.
There is a moment of shift and it is always
present tense. If the body has its gates, perhaps
it also has its culverts, fail-safe routed
by the friendly gesture, the white-flag T,
by the touch that doesn't bruise but tickles:
the older boy inching his fingers lower,
his waistband, lower, his laughter, too,
its pitch and tall-grass sway, ring and yoke, its snort
hot with blood, the bleat of each pleased hiccup, lower.

iii

We will leave them alone for a while, the boys
in empty rooms reciting *truth or dare*
without the question. We will build, instead,
our own mythology. There will be a dark town
fountain filled with honey, sweet fish mouthing

flies from its surface; a blue-winged kookaburra
nesting in the clock tower, pastel eggs
bejeweled with gears; crowds of children
singing beneath a snow, warm, where it lands.
There will be laughter in the trees.

iv

Turn back. One boy has the other in his grip, mouth
crimson with blood. (But which one is the *I*
this poem lays claim to?) I'm asking:
Is it ever the whelp? In the wild? The tiger's
cub who preys on other cubs? Are there stories
for such encounters? Hansel easing Gretel
toward the oven, Gretel not understanding
her sudden urge to burn—

Power, first, like a trick of light
shifting from subject to subject—

See? Already, the story promises to lie.
Power, later, like a hand relinquished to another
hand held in the rain, fingers scrabbling
for purchase. If it's true we're meant to strive,
always, for precision, how come imprecision
most often becomes the focus of the story?
This shtick could go on forever. I guess
I'm reaching for the reason one boy would undress
a younger boy (even here, the betrayal
of relative detail threatens the telling) only to strip,
kneel, and issue the surprising command:
I want you to piss on my back. Power, first
(maybe here, really, first) only a reenactment.
How the younger boy, hard, bewildered, struggled
to aim, splashing the walls, tiles, the older boy's hair,
goddammit, swiveling, *stop*, unable to stop.
How the story seems to say *go ahead*
and laugh; to turn away right at the moment
of discomfort. The moment the older boy rises—

How it seems almost friendly, reaching
for your hand, reader, on a bright day
with no shadows or rain, singing
it happened like this—

SHRINK!

is a word my mother hated / so naturally I hurled it at her / regularly /
I figured all along it wasn't a game / we were playing / the dollhouse
on the table and the box- / cutter in my fist / my mother saying *point* /
to where it happened / saying *cut the room from the house* / *remove it for*
good / except that wasn't exactly / how she put it *let me the fuck in* /
might be more accurate / *shrink!* I'd shout / and I did / I imagined
myself a Playmobil / man small enough I could slip wherever / I wanted
everything / I wanted / gave itself up for me / the underneathness of
things / I cut laminate from particleboard / leather from desk chairs /
found whole worlds / of polyester fibers and wood chips / mulch
minarets / the megalopolis built / from plumbing / stars / sparked by
bad electric / wires black / mold constellations imagine / a house / with
bookend walls / windows glazed with printed paper / sun that hurls
words / onto your bed imagine / the razor edge used to cut your way in
to / every landscape suddenly thick / as a folding screen / smallness that
isn't escape / but subterfuge / imagine / when I finally returned to my
size / returned / to show my mother what I'd found / the smallest crevice
made crevasse / the rooms inside rooms / where it was only me by then /
and the blade

ODE TO MY MOTHER'S TALENT FOR WALKING
IN ON ANY MOVIE DURING THE SEX SCENE;
OR, RUBA'I FOR WHAT RETURNS

The remote control, woefully, fallen to the floor
beyond my reach—we pause: awkward, unsure
how long the scene could possibly last, each breath
drawn in unison, everybody in the room restored
                                        to their body.

PARABLE OF THE MERMAID

Mama claimed it came from the lake.
Fishhooks in its gum line, rot beneath the scales—
I'd say they were frightened, those fishermen

hauling the bladed tail topside, but I know better.
Confused, maybe, to find the fable lifted to life,
filthy, not the portrait they once imagined.

My mama said they kept it in the bathtub: leaky faucet
filling the basin, plumbing concealing its cries. Mama
who puts a cage in every story. Who once told me

New England is all fairy tale. Meaning: Men are always
searching for the miracle they can trap in their trawlers.
Meaning: Don't trust it. I think she once believed

she would die there. I'm aware of her two lives, one spent
kneeling by the water while a minister's hand forced her
under, baptized in submission, *there now, aren't you lovely*,

as, below, a shadow rose—I make too much
of my own imaginings. There's a version of this story
we all know: a woman's voice, her underwater ballad,

calls any brave sailor to her body. And then
there are the fishermen gathered weekly by the tub,
appraising the creature's slowly drying tail, algae-

spotted breath, torso scaled in all the wrong places.
There's a version of this story we all know. They drained
the bath and fed the creature to their sons. My mama

claims she even learned the recipe—enough salt
to taste, to hide the hardtack chew. Mama, who knows
I like my pretty: jeweled ankles, tartan scarves,

a slender arm around my waist. Who I've raised
inside this poem by the lake's white margins,
eyeing each ship, muttering *don't trust it.*

POLICE INTERVIEW AS TWO KNIGHTS OF THE KINGDOM AND A ROGUE ANSWERING THEIR QUESTIONS

And when did this begin?

> Before I wove my voice into cattails. Before my skin mossed over into suede. Before every child became a menace.

And what do you remember most?

> The roaches and rock salt. Dew beads I tried to string on twine around my wrist. How even grubs open when you tickle them.

And where did he touch you?

> I understand how mapmakers begin by charting new discoveries. How land that's always been there reveals itself only by traversing.

And did you like it?

> Maybe you've never danced in shoes that blistered your ankles. Maybe you've never tied a wet rag on your forehead to soothe the sunburnt blemish. Or maybe you're a mess of rash under all that armor.

And where did this transpire?

> The field where every flower was a wick. Every living thing a confusion of flame.

And did his parents know?

> If the road was long, it was also wide, walking what I thought
> was a straight line but could, just as easy, have turned into a
> loop. Gets to the point you don't know a road from a field.
> A house from a home. A friend from something else.

And what did he ask you to do?

> Careful with your coin purse, friend. I know a thing or two
> about drawstrings.

And what did you say?

> The noise two branches make in an early morning wind,
> weighed by birds stepping free from their nests, still light
> enough to shake.

And how did he touch you?

> Do dandelions feel desire? Is there a name for the motion
> their seeds make? That pull?

And were there others?

> *Chucky* and *Jason* and *Freddie*, names you may know from
> their reputation for horror.

And when did this begin?

> After the safe refused to open. The crawlspace, too small to
> hold us both.

And then?

"A GOOD HURT"

is how F. describes the tattoo's needle
even as she dresses, gingerly, her swollen
arm with Neosporin and Glad Wrap.
Look. There's a reason I keep my body

unadorned. You can hear it in the slight
wince of a teenaged girl eating lunch outside
the piercing shop, each mouthful shuffled
past her newly skewered tongue.

Once, a friend asked me to describe
the image of my soul as I perceived it
and I said *jeweled*, which is a pretentious
thing to say, looking back, except—

I used to hoard little secrets stolen
from my schoolmates' hidden lives.
Some alcoholic father returning home, late,
tripping across the slumber party. The dog

found dead with a bone in its throat.
Each talisman sharp in my tongue, I learned
how to lance blood from any ear
with a whisper. I learned the best hurt

is any hurt not my own, as when
I once was offered this choice:
to take the older boy's wire-bound knuckle
to my jaw, or sink my own closed fist

into a smaller boy's ribs. And I turned,
not even needing the reason, the gallery
of onlookers baying an arm's length away,
and lifted the blown-glass paperweight

from the teacher's desk, my arm swinging
into the pinned boy's fluttering frame,
his shoulders hunching to protect the soft
center he wasn't quick enough to hide,

and I felt the wind rush out of him right then
into my fist, into the glass sphere held between
my fingers, with a round hiss of pain I lifted
to my ear and listened to for years, after.

CREATION MYTH

—beginning with line by Joy Harjo

there's no more imagination   we're in it now
         reader   the storm's light rising as a boy

in his father's too-large leather apron
         bends above the factory table   wide as a bed

sheeted and pillowed in the light   his steel rod
         raised through the roof for lightning

to enliven his invention   how clouds cauldron
         and spark   the edges fade   the flash resolves

and now we see it clearly   little bones   little chin
         not yet scarred by acne   a child I guess

except for the flesh-mitten fingers stitched together
         except for the collage of random raccoon

and possum hide patchworking its back
         there is of course the moment of inspection

the boy pinches the child that isn't a child
         flesh that isn't flesh   can't be flesh   those wire-like

hairs already sprouting between the legs that rise
         against his touch   and if I stand here with them

if I watch from the corners of the room   corners
         the light doesn't reach   I'm in this for keeps

after

         the boy tucks his shirt

he steps into the rain
                 left alone the child-thing rises

to test its newfound feet   rubs cocoa butter between its joints
               to hide the smell of musk   wet with what it knows

marks the body as belonging   watch   the light
             shifts   factory lamps dimming as a sun dazzles up

and reader   you should know there are no bystanders
           here   outside the boy snaps his half-split thumbnail

against a matchbook's flint   I pull a ragged tee
           on top my lotioned chest   when I join him

the storm washes smoke from my hair

NO THANKS

—after W. S. Merwin, sort of

listen
        every day the world is making its meager
*mea culpa*s for Easter Peeps arranged on dollar-store plates
        at dinner parties invisible fences the dogs run past
for bleach-stained laundry fresh from the laundromat
        fallen palm leaves whose barbs bloody your fingers
when you sweep them from the road someone somewhere
        is repenting listen it is every living creature's right
to refuse the apology *no thanks* to the vendor
        offering his rhinestone watch before the truck
can tow his trailer from the driveway *I'm good*
        to the postwoman offering whiskey and *who knows*
where it could lead after misplacing another package yes
        god it is good to decline the world its small expressions
of remorse the landlord's handshake as black mold erupts
        from the ceiling the gift basket and wax-armored cheese
after another job falls through the apology you once imagined
        from the boy you last remember as a shape
standing over you naked the shape of all intent
        as you have come to understand it a volition of dark
holy as any power you wrestle with and lose to can be
        holy your neck craning up intending you swear
to reject that single word its rain
        sorry

ACT THREE

CLOUZOT: But surely you agree, M. Godard, that films should have a beginning, a middle part, and an end?

GODARD: Yes, but not necessarily in that order.

—Interview, Cannes International Film Festival, 1966

YOU KEEP ASKING THE QUESTION.
WE KEEP ANSWERING.

Mama made a batch of blueberry pancakes
that day. I remember the dough

stuck to every surface—
Mama? What Mama. I had friends.

I mean boys. There were three of us—
five of us—

two—
one of them in particular.

At that age *one* can be many.
I owned a teal Schwinn, rusted—

scooter with motorized carriage—
I would ride even if the tires were flat.

He knew every back alley and cut.
The empty apartment two blocks over,

its windows easy to open.
Builders never finished the sash.

Mama packed me a lunch of ham sandwich—
egg salad and onion—

peanut butter—
potato chips between the bread.

I remember thinking *sash*
was a nice sounding word—

The first time I came
it felt like a window breaking.

And I was the window.
And I was the fist—

I kept repeating that one word,
silent, in my head. *Sash.*

I might have muttered it once.
It might have sounded like *yes.*

It was sunny.
I mean cloudy—

I don't remember the weather—
It was always hot—

Safe bet, it was hot.
I might have said that once. *It's hot.*

You don't understand context at that age.
Context is everything. What the fuck

does that even mean to a first grader—
I didn't cry about it. He once said *tool.*

As in *you don't know how to use yourself.*
I do—

I went to see *Aladdin on Ice!* with his parents—
My parents took us to the movies—

They chaperoned us in—
They dropped us at the curb—

We walked the same path to school
each morning. Those back alleys, again.

We learned about saturation in science class.
How, eventually, a rag dipped in water

just won't hold any more.
Is this too plain—

Am I saying it clearly—
What's too much, too many—

I'm afraid of the saturation point, my story
like a rag you can't use to clean any damn thing.

Hard, mostly, to admit it was another kid—
Hard? Yes I was hard—

I believed in the word *stoic*. Dead last in second-grade
vocabulary but I clung to my few words—

I was spelling bee champ. Mouth like a prize.
He'd put it on my tongue and say *spell*

my name—
My name, a question in Mama's mouth:

that's how I knew she knew—
Pops caught on first—

I had two fathers. One, brand new. One,
old, living off bourbon and canned tea.

C'mere and rub my shoulder.
How'd you get so good at that—

Stoic—
Sash—

I lied about the fists. He never hit me—
He hit me once—

He slung coins at my ribs. He called me
wishing well. I wished a lot

until I learned what prayer was.
I prayed for it to end—

I prayed for it to keep going—
Hard, mostly, to admit I was seven—

they were ten—
I'd just turned five—

he was fifth grade, held back—
I was nine when words became

the empty apartment I live in today.
It's not like it fucked me up for life—

We played a lot of *Go Fish.* I hid cards
up my sleeve. I liked to win. I think about that

sometimes. You know, winning. What that meant
to me. *Fish* rhymed with *wish. Go wish*—

Why would I come forward?
It wasn't like he was my teacher—

parent—
neighbor—

He was my neighbor. He liked trivia.
Do you know what sex means? I spelled it.

I thought it meant something
like blueberry pancakes—

I remember he windowed a girl. I mean
invited. I mean she never came over—

She came over once—
We went to her place—

There was an attic, cold—
That's what I remember most

about the basement. Wanting
and not wanting. Not like it mattered.

It was always hot. I'd get chills anyway.
Goose pimples. I remember lying on the floor—

couch—
braided rug—

looking at the rafters' warped beams
and, between them, pink

tufts of foam insulation that looked to me
like flesh. New flesh. Impossible

to turn away from. Bulbous. Doughing.
I mean bulging. You know,

wet. Gleaming.
Always there in the dark.

Until I found myself reaching for it.
Just to touch. To know. Surprised

to find it brittle, hollow,
not at all warm—

If I came, I didn't have a word for it—
We threw footballs on the street.

Once, I cracked his window
into pieces. That's not a metaphor, exactly—

The city was quaint—
I hated the city. Big. Old.

Nothing to do but rag rocks.
I mean kick—

It's not like you could call it rape—
He was a kid, I was a kid—

I don't believe in excuses—
Pleasure. Now there was a word

with coins in it. I learned to spell that one
later in life. Nickels and quarters

falling free. Mouth like a prize—
The truth is I loved

the ice rink—
movie theater—

sitting in the back row—
dead last—

I haven't used the word *body.*
How my body liked the thrill.

I mean chill. I mean
how edges resolve in the dark

until the curtain falls,
the house lights come up—

I mean, you know.

ACT FOUR

My questions were not original.
Nor did I answer them.

—Anne Carson, "The Glass Essay"

ON LEAVING DETROIT FOR LOS ANGELES

face it: there's something romantic about being left behind,
isn't there? if god once spoke through wild iris and foliage, they
(for how could they *not* be plural) have since given up the ghost.
ragged edges, scorch-bottomed pots. (there is praise everywhere,

isn't there?) if god once spoke through wild iris and foliage, they
drag their tongue, now, through rust and metal shavings.
(ragged edges. scorch-bottomed pots.) there is praise, everywhere.
(try again. be specific.) once, to be closer to danger or my blood

i dragged my tongue through rust and metal shavings.
i broke inside the tumbledown hotel, staged photos with its ruins—
try again. be specific. once, to be closer to danger, my blood
split a continent in two. who wouldn't swap

the broken insides of a tumbledown hotel (staged photos, silly ruins)
for a city with stars etched in its sidewalks? (city, wide as a
split continent.) tell me. who wouldn't swap
tarnished scrap for a gold link chain worn beneath the collar?

for a city with stars etched in its sidewalks, city wide as a
graveyard with nothing left to mark the gone
but tarnished scrap? (the gold link chain beneath my collar
inviting god's tongue, closer.) everyone knows the story

of a graveyard, its nothings left to mark those gone.
(for how could they *not* be plural?) those given up. those ghosts
inviting god's tongue, closer. (everyone knows this story.)
face it. there's something romantic about being left behind,

isn't there?

ODE TO THE COMMUNITY GARDEN, WHICH IS REALLY JUST A VACANT LOT BETWEEN APARTMENT BUILDINGS; OR, ON SPENDING MY LAST UNEMPLOYMENT CHECK

Praise the empty garden, its free admission and tip jar.
The buzzards picking at their leftovers
of chipmunk or mouse rot don't care

about my T-shirt shrunk too small in the wash,
the newly purchased scarf I couldn't afford
but fuck it. The economy of consumption

is everywhere. Look. The hawk eats the fox
and that is a loss. The fox eats the squirrel
and that is a loss. The squirrel buries the acorn

and that is an investment in future acorns.
Recently, while interviewing for the job
I thought I wanted, a wealthy filmmaker

compared poverty to *not buying a lemonade*
with your fast food dinner. Later that same day
(you can see it coming, can't you?)

he bought me a lemonade. At what point
does a gesture of kindness become
some other kind of gesture?

      When I was ten or twelve,
           when my father slammed our last
      carton of milk against the—

When the repo men arrived in—

      My father, the gentlest man I—

            Two flashlights through the windows,
exposing furniture, bare, in the dark, where—

      And I was not ashamed, am not ashamed,
            to say *ashamed* would not be—

      When, years later, the woman I love
calls from work to ask about my walk,
        how it was, if any of the usual figures
            appeared, the buzzards, or—

When even the tail end of her braided hair
            in the wind begins to resemble a price—

Am I damaged in some essential way?
Striding through the garden
with all the purpose I can muster,

the purpose a body manufactures
when it stops to lift the lily, its petals,
thinking: I could hold this

until all the water drains from my palms.
Wondering
        how much?

"I TREAT MY MONEY LIKE MY SIDE HO."

For all the languages I struggle to speak—
among them French, the romantic's
tongue, which I studied for six years
before nearly failing my final semester
in college, hiring a Parisian ex-pat in love
with Jamiroquai and Motown as my tutor,
and turning it all around on my exams
only to have the few words I managed to collect
fall from my open mouth for good—
money is the language I struggle with most.
Bank statements. Tax filings. Direct
deposit dropping into my bottom line
like sleet in June, forever unexpected.
For years I would say, of my finances,
if I don't look at it, it isn't real, which is hardly
a winning policy for any long-term relationship.
When searching for advice, my friend freely
tells me: *I treat my money like my side ho. I had to
make it something I adored, something I needed
and couldn't get rid of. Something that demanded
I develop a strategy to keep.* Ever since
she's managed her assets meticulously.
Though the love may be wicked, controlling,
so what? I take her advice to heart. I purchase
the second phone, pay-as-you-go, with minutes
easy to replenish by anonymous credit
and put H&R Block on speed dial. I create
separate email accounts with obscure screen names
and randomly generated passwords. At night
I hoard each envelope spirited from the mailbox,
pored over in low light, later locked in cabinets full
of fevered correspondence. I am constantly afraid
to admit how badly I want this. A few months in

I buy myself expensive gifts because I understand
it's my job to keep the thrill alive. Persian towels.
Parisian bath salts. (Enough French left
to read the label.) I call my accountant. We speak
in patois full of code, a lexicon of addition,
subtraction, actuarial tables of unfulfilled desire,
which is one way of saying: I nearly cry on the phone,
every time, with the gratitude of a foreign traveler
finally able to read the signage, to find
their way back to the lover that waits for them.
But which one? My friend tells me
there's nothing wrong with a ho though I see
how furtive it's made me. Though
I've begun repeating the words *dalliance,*
paramour, like incantations beneath my breath.
When my wife comes home from another day
at the hospital, shift-tired, grateful for the gift
of my open arms to wrap her in embrace—
I fall in love again. This is the romance
of risk and reward: how every ordinary
detail enlivens with what's at stake.
The braise bubbling in its Dutch oven.
A pair of pajamas, bunched on the floor.
The letters—from my bank, the state,
tax boards demanding compliance—
pressed against the seams of their hiding place.
Even this, I treasure. How they threaten
to burst free. To give it all away.

AMBITION

the son of an insomniac, i'm practiced at hearing the little
bells of a restless night ring before arrival. how the cut

angle of my neighbor's porch light knifes past slat blinds
in slants to remind me, somewhere, the world is hard

at work. whole years i learned to roll shut the factory doors
of my eyes, to seal out the city's soundings, asleep, until

i found myself again leaning in the half-open door
of my mind. its neon cravings screamed the night

awake. it may sound predictable but i never understood,
given time, the heart's hunger will eat even the body.

it may seem obvious to say it but, given practice,
the body's dark streets will learn to echo back

night's province of pawn shops, windows full of treasure,
hand-scrawled ads promising salvation for the price

of a few keepsakes. at this dim threshold i've haunted
too many times, too dull for the drunk or delirious to find

comfort, where billboards mouth their horseshit vows
and wind labors to lift each breath at my shirtsleeve,

i'm practiced at bending low to the jewel cases until
even my mud brown eyes become gems looped with string

and it's not romantic, the way daylight breaks the color
of bullion on this street. magpies shriek the day

awake. laundromats open their damp mouths
to gargle with coins.

TO THE SOCIAL MEDIA INFLUENCER IN LINE
AHEAD OF ME AT STARBUCKS

I wasn't watching when you pulled the phone
          from your pocket fired up the camera
held it overhead to proclaim *Yo I'm here at Starbucks*
          on Melrose with these fly ass Angelenos

so maybe that's on me but the fact is I was caught
          by surprise when you turned the lens
behind you *smile motherfucker* and I mooned
          dumb as a cow in its stall for the screen

I moved to Los Angeles for familiar reasons
          the truth is I was once an accomplished
child actor performing well-adjusted
          cheer for my parents

I remember calling my house
          a *black box theater* as only an only
child with an active
          imagination might call it

it is difficult to describe now
          this feeling of always being watched
protective sure but also I don't know
          expectant the way one watches

a pot of water before it boils
          a morning glory half-wilted
on its stem the moment the sun peeks up
          and you hope for the damned thing

to open I haven't
            spoken to my family in weeks
spoken I mean in the manner of families
            on television all breezy dialogue

and so I label every customer in the café
            mother and *father* I imagine
each corner table carefully set with place mats
            each latté a casserole we lean over

and spoon one another platefuls of dinner
            all of it bluntly wholesome
the mothers and fathers not yet
            training their cyclopean eye

on the child they fear
            they've failed the violent action
now all backstory each new detail
            rife with danger the child

now and always held in their sight
            even at a distance even through the eyes
of a customer in some California Starbucks
            staring with barely concealed interest

as the internet celebrity
            having made the rounds
returns to try me once more
            how about that smile

and see how easy it can be to be
            the morning glory
just for a second to imagine
            your family somewhere

flipping channels in the ether
        finding you there on the screen
wondering if you will do
        what they have always hoped

if you are going to wave
        if you are going
to smile and cry and thank them
        for watching

GOOGLE KNOWS LITERALLY EVERYTHING ABOUT YOU—HERE'S HOW TO DELETE THAT DATA

—HuffPost UK, March 28, 2018

it would be so much easier to erase a person
        in the conventional sense   *did you mean*

sun exposure   *did you mean*   gun shows
        did you mean   a dark lake after nightfall

it sounds unconvincing to say *kill it*
        however you can   but how else are you supposed to

understand your own resilience   servers
        somewhere   hoarding photos of you   your love

outside that cobblestone café   the threatening email
        sent to the classmate you hated in high school

see you in the parking lot   really   there's nothing
        wrong with this version of yourself

not wrong with you now   32 searches for *how to treat*
        ingrowns   followed by 45 minutes of GIF porn

set to private   *why do I find punishment sexy*
        is only one query you never really answer

can coffee lower your libido   *can coffee really give you cancer*
        coffee   *health benefits*   remember

there have been miracles of disappearance across human
        history   *what happened to*   Amelia Earhart

Jimmy Hoffa   *those ships in the Bermuda Triangle*   still
        your face comes swimming back

when summoned   *third-grade class portraits*   *throwback!*
          accept you will suffer

losses   ignore the mute apparitions that surface
          when you scrub the network for your name

the boys   their bowl cuts   fat cheeks and smiles
          you remember differently   it's only ego

that says you don't recognize this mirror   *at what age*
          does a person acquire agency   is pleasure

ever involuntary   take a Sharpie
          to every screen you own

black them out   what lasts beyond you
          is beyond you

why is my breath heaviest before climbing into bed
          what does it mean to want and want

and never feel sated   how does a person ever learn
          to trust the good intentions

of children   forget the body   forget
          the body you once wanted so badly

to lose   light your candles   lie down
          inside your growing assemblage

of questions   *did you mean*
          there will be no other gods

did you mean
          there will be no other lives

after   anymore

PARABLE OF THE GOLEM

I knew the risks, what tales had been told, the blueprints
labeled *Danger*. When I laid the first strands of copper
in its clay, engraved my name's spell on its forehead, was I

frightened? I knew: to unmake what had been gifted, partial
mistake of happenstance, equal measures salt and soft and soft—
I had to build myself an Other. There is no word for

the tender rush of rust warmed with breath, eyes of fuse-
blown bulbs blinkered by flash, the specter of all one's fears
whetted sharp. Upon awakening, the figure couldn't speak,

only mouth my giving flesh against its bone-saw teeth. I understood,
then, *tenderness* did not mean *gentle*. I did not know how to build
something functional, unbroken, had only ever learned to fix

but not create. Its limbs were badly bound with twine. It creaked
when it limped, rattletrap head hung from its sway—
and so? When it took me in its arms, I could feel it fumble

for the loose bolt in my joints, seams in need of solder,
handful of nails probing for flaws. It believed I was perfectible.
With each passing day, it braided foil in my hair. Wove

wire between my teeth. It did not view such totems as *beauty*
but *protection*. It, too, swelled. Lattice-fence armor, legs lumber-
braced. Can you see it? Gangly frame, stooped? Somehow lovely?

When it brought me the pieces of my enemies, I did not shrink
from the sight. What did you expect? I would erase my name
from its doings? No. Like a mother to her child, I pulled

the creature's head to my shoulder, where I drew
the knife sheathed in my boot and leaned
into its earthen flesh to carve

each letter, deeper.

ODE TO XERISCAPING; OR, REGARDING AUSTERITY, I FIND DEVOTION

When the agave slices
        your naked knee, praise
the little blood it leaves

        there. Do not wish
for rain. There are shapes
        thirst makes of the body

and each is a kind of knife:
        breathing barb, living blade.
Praise the water shaming

        protestors camped outside
the sloping lawns,
        the overfed greenery

too sumptuous to trust. The knee
        socks and work boots
you purchased just to armor

        for our walks—
Darling. We have moved
        from a city with rusted rebar

blooming from coal ash
        to a city with plant
life lathed sharp by need

        and what does that say
about the way I sometimes drag
        the razor across my face

at just the wrong angle.
        I press my teeth
against your neck

        the moment I push inside you.
I squeeze your fingers to my palm
        tight enough to sting.

Praise now the landscape—
        how it cuts, forcing
our tangled legs closer

        as we walk. Do not begrudge
a single drop of blood. Let the dirt
        take its taste. Tell the land

it must wait to have the rest of you.

SURVIVAL GUIDE FOR GREAT INDOORSMEN

In San Bernardino State Park, six thousand feet
above sea level, a place so remote
no one would notice for weeks if I went
casually, almost easily missing, I hitch
a stoic smile to my face and hike the winter trail
ten paces out front, my friends, warm in their fleece-
lined vests and laughter, allowing me to lead, when I see,
in the snow, nearly the same size as my overlarge
Timberland boots, a paw print, and because
I'm not an alarmist, because I don't want to scream
the word *bear!* because I can't bear to hear
my own voice stripped high in the altitude,
I shout: "Guys! I think I found something!"
In California, any hike is rife with risk
of wildlife encounters. Mountain lion. Brown bear.
Rattlesnake. Swimming is no better. To swim
in the ocean is to reenter the food chain. Tiger
shark. Great white shark. Portuguese man o'war.
Hammerhead shark. Jellyfish. Fishing trawlers
whose nets, broken from their pulleys, float
like invisible snares to hook unsuspecting
paddlers. Oil spills. You get the gist.
I once heard a teacher refer to himself
as *a great indoorsman* and have considered
getting the words tattooed on my bicep
ever since. It's fortunate, for those like us,
there are guides full of practical instructions
for survival. In case of a mountain lion: get big.
In case of a rattlesnake: stand still.
In case of a bear: play dead. Unless the bear
is startled, mating, with cubs. Unless the snake
initiates the dance. Unless the lion has decided,
at that particular hour, nothing is larger

than hunger. I'm not saying my fear makes sense.
I'm saying the bear you don't see is more terrifying
than the bear you do. Or not. A bear,
like Niagara Falls, lives up to its reputation
for awe. Sometimes two truths coexist.
Truth: I watched *Grizzly Man* in high school
and dreamt for weeks afterward in the same
key of two documentarians being eaten alive.
Truth: It's peaceful in the mountains. I escape
there as often as I can. In Los Angeles
solitude requires commitment. I cultivate
my own ecosystem. I've learned to avoid
my neighbors, the peering eyes of baristas,
friendly though they may be. I remain confined
to my apartment, my car, my littlest village
of screens. Even here, what's wild presses in.
In case of user Snowflake_KillR_1980
cursing you by name in the comments section
of some CSPAN newsclip posted to social media:
block them. In case of a truck on the highway
honking behind you, high beams flashing with ire:
slow to let them pass. In case of a man at your door
hawking flyers that gleefully proclaim *The End
of Days*, his fist banging, actually banging the screen
for you to open, already, accept the bitter
sacrament of reality: carefully latch the deadlock.
Leave his howl to the roadside, some poor sedan
perpetually stuck in idle. Unless the man decides,
right then, to strike down all non-believers.
Unless the truck nudges your bumper. Unless
the fascist in the comments section doxes
your address, sourced from public domain
registries, to an e-blast of trolls. Unless
you no longer know where the threat is
coming from. Spindrift cycle of menace.
Confusion of jeopardy. In San Bernardino
State Park, the trees are all half-burned—
a memory of fire. Lampblack bark charred

limbless, root to trunk, until: Green
buds. Bird nests. Bear paw. Look
how I call the imagined creature to my palm.
How it shivers with pleasure, the way animals
sometimes do, and walks beside me down
the wintry trail, leaving only our single
set of tracks behind.

SPARE RIB WITH SHIITAKE SLAW AND SCALLION GLAZE

—for Tina

The rib between my fingers
    for a long moment, dripping

        with au jus and aioli, when
    you ask: *Should I leave you two alone?*

You shoo me from the frame
    to snap a glam-shot of my plate

        before it's cleared, and I wonder:
    Are we this alike? Do you fear

losing what you have more than enjoying
    what arrives? Always I save the best

        bite for last, this bite, always, turned cold—
    I'm trying to explain

why I took three years to say the words
    I love you. Why a boy like me never spit

        blood licked from lips split
    in winter, never stood beneath the storm

to drink its rain for fear of the funnel
    forming in his throat, a boy

        who kept his jaws clamped shut
    even when a girl laid him gently

on the floor to press a Hershey's
    Kiss against his lips—

let me try again. A child learns
early in life the mouth does not give back,

to taste means to consume, and who, having eaten
their fill, doesn't eventually mourn

the meal? Curled steam flushing
the cheeks, cayenne and chilies blazing

thatched timbers in the mouth.
Who hasn't played *No, you*

hang up in attempt to prolong
the tin can whisper of a voice

wavering on the phone and threatening
even then, from a distance, to fold

upon itself, somehow smaller,
diminished? This is a song

the tongue knows. The tongue, wet
with loneliness and glue, that parses

parsimony and sage, poblano
and pear, coils of anise-studded orange

brewed in a dark coffee. And the words
we feed one another.

Unctuous. Sour.
Love. Come.

Be alone with me
to savor what arrives

and is gone.

ACT FIVE

you realize it is all your body now, everything between you
& the pieces you lost once, the towers & crows,
the city (you) gleaming
in long, glorious hyphen

—Aracelis Girmay, "Portrait of the Woman as a Skein"

LET LOOSE AT LUNCH, THE BOYS IMAGINE

what they cannot understand: rumble of machinery
and hellfire, wreckage sieving palm leaves, puddles. Or:
gunmetal iced with fingerprints, chill fog against the sea.
The boys, their not-so-imaginary army, crawling for

the countertops, the bathrooms, Formica flecked like snow.
I was one of them once. Boy starred with scattershot scree.
Boy with fanged sneakers, soles sharp with broken glass. For
what? He couldn't understand. The rumble of machinery

claimed him as its own. Not a boy, but grist fallen free
from lathe and wheel. Not the furnace, but beetles stormed
beneath its coals, shells he hollowed into beads.
Hellfire, wreckage sieving palm leaves, puddles—war

made sense of the body. How he opened like a door
rusted at the lock, resistant even to the lovers he
invited in. How evenings, in their hands, he became more
gunmetal iced with fingerprints, chill fog against the sea.

There are some struggles too great to recount. Limbs kneeled
in dark gauze. Stippled constellations of lamplight on a floor.
Later he will learn there is no thrill greater than surrender, freed
from the boys, their not-so-imaginary army, crawling toward

his every move. His hands, not metal, not made only for
what cuts. Little wrath riddled with exit wounds—see?
Buried in sandbox foxholes, bunkered under chairs: the corps
takes aim, thumbs cocked, ready to fire on or flee

what they cannot understand.

ROAST!

Kid! Your feet are so ugly *even the sky hides*
from your toenails. *You wear Crocs*

and the sun comes out *to thank you.*
Your emails so long *the computer falls*

asleep. So literal *you thought a quarterback*
was a refund. O friends. I have

never mastered this particular power of talking
shit. I understand there's spark to it.

I've spent years striking tinder against
my teeth, tumbling pebbles on the palate.

Always my words fall heavy. Dull. Friends.
I've spent years blistering in your affection

each gentle melted and reshaped sharp
as in: *You're so scrawny* *you look like a coatrack*

your parents dressed *at BigNTall.* Meaning:
I know *your mama bought you that shirt*

from Kohl's on discount *three sizes too large. Here.*
I have a spare. Wear it *as long as you need.*

As in: *Your voice so nasal* *you sound like a toilet*
your daddy clogged *with bourbon shits.* Meaning:

I can hear the snot rattling in your throat *sorrow-sick*
or sick-sick *one sometimes leading to the other. Don't wipe*

your nose with one-ply   *from the stall. Rest your head*
on my chest. I don't mind   *the damp.* All along

I thought we were playing   with flame.
Having been burned   I meant to burn back. As in:

You're so thirsty you'll wind up like your father   *whole lake*
of liquor dammed   *behind the teeth. Your wife and children*

drown in you. Maybe   I got the rules fucked up, heat
all wrong, friends I'm speaking now   only to you.

You've homaged my fat   tongue, stubby
tongue, tongue   that can't curl a curse

for shit. You've named me   *pimple-winged*
angel, Bacne Batman, scalded me   in every tender

so I might never bleed there   again. Friends.
You declare each day   warm, bright, while

I'm left to my usual labor   knocking rocks
in the dirt, breaking   each one hollow

as eggshells. Their big mouths   open. Their big
open mouths   empty as ever.

MANIFESTO WITH HONEY AND BULLETS

So you must not be frightened . . . when a sorrow
rises up before you, greater than you have ever
seen . . .

—Ranier Maria Rilke

In 2013, scientists exhumed thirty canopic jars filled with honey
from a pharaoh's tomb in Egypt. I'm told honey can last indefinitely
if stored in a properly sealed container. To cleanse the sucrose

bees regurgitate nectar from one mouth to another. They deposit
the half-digested fluid in a wax-lined chamber. It is almost tender,
this process: one insect's proboscis pressed to another's. Have you ever

stared down a tunnel wondering what lay at its conclusion?
Elsewhere, at a theater in Aurora, Colorado, a stranger walks
into the audience (his brief silhouette, contained) and opens

fire on its viewers. A man walks into a grade school and opens
fire on its students. A man walks into a church and opens
fire on its congregants. These are just some of the stories

I would like history to regurgitate. Colony Collapse Disorder
is what academics call the slow disintegration of the honey bee's
organized community without explanation. Today,

in Hanyuan County, roving bands of farmers pollinate fields
by Q-tip—rubber-gloved fingers dusted with pollen.
Imagine: an entire year's crops dependent on a plastic bag

split at the corners. Do they rub the powder on their gums?
The furniture? Do they smear the meager few dollars stuffed
in their pockets? Everything, suddenly, filled with the opportunity

to become more of itself. I sometimes wonder
if Death is one property we seek to make more of.
There are stories and there are stories. It is rumored

Alexander the Great had his body embalmed in honey.
The gun used by George Zimmerman to kill Trayvon Martin
sold for thousands of dollars in an online auction.

Which of these tales seems astonishing depends on your position
in history. Honey contains the enzyme glucose oxidase
which produces hydrogen peroxide. It was once routine practice

to use honey as a common disinfectant. Bullets can be purchased
in multiple iterations. *Hollow Tip. Soft Point. Tracer.*
They are considered ineffective as medical implements. In 2016

police officers fatally shot Alton Sterling while pinning his arms
to the sidewalk. That Alton Sterling was Black and in Louisiana
are what certain white communities might call *anecdotal details.*

When I say certain white communities I mean all white communities
must reckon with themselves. Did you know honey can be found
in three hundred varietals? *Alfalfa, Bassswood, Fireweed, Tupelo.* I find

these names indescribably lovely. After another shooting, a friend
combats her helplessness by filling notebooks with a litany of dead.
She tells me: *I find this list indescribably lacking.* Egyptians believed

in commemorating history with language. I have to believe
hope lives in a wax-sealed chamber. Why else write this?
The average worker bee will produce up to one-twelfth teaspoon

of honey in her lifetime should she live long enough to see it
through. When scientists sampled the centuries-old nectar
they agreed it was good. That was the word they used.

Good. Once, I put a bullet casing in my mouth
expecting it to taste of metal or scorched powder.
But it didn't. I tongued the hollow shell clean.

It didn't taste like anything.

KINK

as in the bent link between words
        how *sex* leads to *sects* to *sectioned* to

the lobster boiled with lemongrass and bay leaf
        split on my dinner plate

the way *umami* sounds like a pleasure cry
        cut loose in the kitchen

praise or don't but allow yourself to open
        for the fork in the sea urchin's shell

pulsing even after it's split *offal*
        fried with capers their pretty names

sweetbreads concealing glands that fold beneath the fork
        we hold our breath before the first bite

mean to or not how lovely the percussive
        grunts that mark consumption

heat anything long enough it loses its form
        flame that coaxes layers of flavor

from collagen and cartilage marrow sloughing
        from bones halved and broiled

the cooking twine that fastens Sunday's roast
        shrinking tighter below

the bubbled skin love how good to feel
        this craving stretch the rope of me

and you tie it

ARS POETICA AS LOVE POEM WITH
AUTO-CORRECT; OR, MISSION YOU

We're far enough into the future
        what I call night
light might also mean the dozen or so

          screens that brighten my living
room furniture. Far enough, what I mean by
        death might also be the slow

replacement of my hands, the way they tremor
        when I laugh, by photos that live
on a server somewhere in Arizona, each

          hard drive filled with theaters I rotate
in the dark, smiling. I admit
        there are days I require language

to make my body in the world feel real;
        days I walk headlong into my words
and find nothing I recognize there.

          Not the goose-like form of shoes
stormed against the door. Not the shape of bed
        quilts left by morning's hurried departure.

Shit, we're far enough into the future
        there should be a word by now to say
I have unsubscribed from this email chain

          on ten separate occasions and now
I am prepared to break my phone. A second
        word for the thousand-and-one times

I have tried to unsubscribe from that feeling
        I sometimes get between my toes
after a long run, numbness I'm silently terrified

        means nerve damage. Or maybe
we're far enough now from our bodies,
        our landscapes, we've lost lexicon

to faithfully describe the ocotillo: how it sprouts
        from the desert like hair
from the dead. How the desert stretches

        out and out until, finally,
the distance between myself
        and the world no longer seems

so strange. The idea of leaving it, now,
        no stranger than the word *abacus*
meaning a beaded string scholars once used

        to tally up their days. Far,
whatever, but maybe not so far
        language can't still keep me—

the surprise of my phone's corrective mind,
        how *missing you* becomes *mission you*
and there it is: accuracy. The body

        I've waited for. Body (yours)
I need. One small toe reaching
        farther than its neighbors.

Fat tumor blooming below the shoulder
        that I kiss to keep well-loved
and benign. You, magpie comedian

laughing in your mother's voice.
You, house plant empath gently
misting their leaves. You.

Objective and journey. Obstacle.
Reward. Our future blinks by,
surprising and mundane, and look

how far we've come, you and I,
needing only the word our feet make
as they walk side by side.

UNCORRECTED ERROR

How many times have you made this same mistake,
willing, always, to be wrong, to step dumb into daylight
as you shuffle down the sidewalk toward the high school
just let out, its circus of sneakers and skateboards stomping
your feet
              when some man across the street raises
his hand to wave, mouth forming the shape of your one
good name, calling you over, friend, love, and you, smiling,
known, raise your own five fingers, waving back, all
solitude's sapphires fallen from your collar—

until a second figure jostles past to take your place, to take
the hand held out in welcome, wearing their name
shaped like yours, their obvious relief at finding
a familiar face to rupture the day's well-lit loneliness
like yours, like you,
                stranger?

ODE TO GRIFFITH PARK; OR, EVERY TOURIST
ATTRACTION GIVES ME ANOTHER REASON
FOR MISTRUST

We were walking along the cliff-edge
trail where, above, the planetarium
squinted into smog, the smog

which smelled, even there, of car exhaust
but which you said you liked
to think was really a collection of exhalations

made by the weary and ambitious
wandering the city's hiking paths,
when a man, his two dogs, rounded the corner.

That sudden blow: familiarity. A face
distorted by years but also, somehow, *same*.
Had I heard he moved here? Had I heard—

it was the dogs who knew me first,
who knew the quivered hitch in my steps
and what that meant. I should say

this was not the first time his face appeared
unannounced. Once, in a glass of milk
left overnight on the counter. Once,

on the drive-thru screen large as any horizon
I refuse to drive toward. And once, I dreamt
I carried his sleeping figure, still a boy, to drop

from the highway overpass. Dreamt
he forced another naked child
to their knees to show me

what he wanted
only it wasn't a dream—
what happened next?

      Did we pass each other—
           Did he wave, pretending not to—
    Friendly, *hello*—

            Did the dogs strain at—
        The sun unburdened—
      Hikers pausing or passing—

I guess I'll never know. I lied
about certain details: the man's
appearance, his dogs, the whole

sorry episode. The truth is
I am so often blinded by my friends
pulling back their shirt collar, or skirt

hem, or boot to point at the brilliant,
glowing wound. Which is maybe, only,
another way of saying I would be happy

to give away my own. To forfeit my anticipation
of the man's arrival at any waking moment.
It wasn't all a lie. I refuse to exclude joy.

We were walking the path that day.
The city yawned below us. You took
my hand, going on about lonesomeness,

how lucky we were, together.

ANOTHER DIORAMA, REVISED

It happened like this—

With no shadows or rain, singing
for your hand, reader, on a bright day.
Here, the story seems almost friendly,
reaching from discomfort, from
the moment the older boy rises—

And laughs. And turns away right
as the song seems to say *go ahead
goddammit.* And then: *stop—*

The younger boy, hard, bewildered, struggling
(maybe here, really, first) only as reenactment.
I want you to step to the back. Power, now,
kneeling to obey the surprising command
of specific detail; to alter the telling; to strip
the younger boy, even here, of betrayal.
I'm reaching for the reason one boy would undress—

This shtick could go on forever. I guess,
most often, forgiveness become the focus of the story.
Always, chasing precision. Always, imprecision
gaining purchase. If it's true we're meant to strive
for wholeness, for the hand held in the rain,
power, yes, relinquished to another—

See? Already the story promises to lie,
shifting from subject to subject. So?
Power, at last, just a trick of light—

PALINODE

God, even the dirt here smells
like diesel and used condoms.
You expected transfiguration,
some lawnmower revealing
the land's essential shape, buzzards
recycling a field's forgotten trash.
Why is it gratitude so often feels curated?
How good, to trap the neighborhood
possum in a cage and see fear paling
its face. I will build no sanctuary
with these hands. I will not clasp them
in worship. But I will hold the hot mug
while you wait for it to cool, the pan
above its fire. There *are* transfigurations.
Forget the meadow. If there is
a burning—here. Each day
I learn to hold some new shape
of flame. Why expect anything
else, after?

THE COOKOUT

—after Jason Shinder

That's how it goes. The meal ends, all of us
scraping the plates of our loneliness

into the dishwater. I hug my friends goodnight.
I don't take special notice of the way

Priscila's elbow clicks when it bends, how
Bash's collarbone juts into my neck. I close

the door behind them, and just like that:
the virus. Just like that: months of video calls,

I pray this email finds you in hopeful spirits.
That's how it goes. What arrives arrives

suddenly. I disinfect the groceries. I sit
on the toothsome couch. I blur days with days

on television. It is a story with very little action.
When I was still a boy, my parents would cruise

around suburban streets singling out houses—
What about that one? We could repaint the siding—

we would never be able to afford. It didn't matter.
I stretched my little legs across the car seat

like a couch, made a TV of my Gameboy.
I bay windowed the moon roof. I pitied

the others, those kids with backyard swimming
pools and *au pair*s, who didn't know this augury—

this homing the night, our own. Today
I cul-de-sac the sugar packets strewn

on my dining table. I stretch the afghan
above the bed, its threadbare blue skying

with lamplight. Friends, I imagine the cookout
we'll have here. I roof my hands. I picket

my teeth. I lawn and lawn the tongue for any
who need to rest. Come through!

Bring the beer, Mike. Will, help yourself
to the barbeque. Tom, Jake, you're in charge

of margaritas. Quit asking, Kevin. Of course
you can bring the dog. Come in, Sam. Come in, Fati.

Hieu, goddamn, let me try on those glasses. Andrés!
Put the little ones on the carpet. Driss is here.

With Cynthia! There by the hearth, Mary Anne
nursing her mug of cocoa, having found

unlikely companions in Chris and Gina. Listen to them
yammering about the news. Tina, darling, you know

these halls better than any. Crank up the speakers,
never mind the neighbors. V, I've saved

a blanket special for your shoulders. Tell Matthew
he doesn't have to worry. Stop tidying the counter,

Van. Brandon, you too. My parents will be here
any moment. Dan's on his way. Are you

surprised he forgot the time? I have to name them
you understand. I have to name them to understand

they're here. That's how it goes. We home whatever
we have. Even the body. Especially

the body. And although it is already sundown
in the world of this poem, although the doors

are opening, the guests again making excuses,
streaming into a dark I am no longer certain

we will ever step out from—
here are their dishes. Here is the water

dirty with signs of their living.

ACKNOWLEDGMENTS

Many thanks to the editors of the following publications in which a number of these poems first appeared, sometimes in different versions:

The Account: "Creation Myth" ("There's no more imagination")

Beloit Poetry Journal: "Kink"

Cortland Review: "Insect Life of Michigan"

Fairy Tale Review: "Let loose at lunch, the boys imagine" and "Parable of the Mermaid"

Four Way Review: "Killer of Sheep"

Frontier Poetry: "Ars Poetica as Love Poem with Auto-Correct; or, Mission You"

Gettysburg Review: "Home Remedy"

Indiana Review: "Parable of the Golem"

Leon Literary Review: "Ambition" and "Shooter"

Missouri Review: "Ode to the Community Garden, Which Is Really Just a Vacant Lot between Apartment Buildings; or, On Spending My Last Unemployment Check"

North American Review: "Ode to Xeriscaping; or, Regarding Austerity, I Find Devotion" and "Palinode" ("God, even the dirt here smells")

POETRY: "No Thanks"

Prairie Schooner: "Ode to Griffith Park; or, Every Tourist Attraction Gives Me Another Reason for Mistrust"

Redivider: "No matter how many times I pass"

RHINO Poetry: "Spare Rib with Shiitake Slaw and Scallion Glaze"

Shallow Ends: "Ode to Hydrangeas Ending in Reflection on a Childhood Visit from the Emergency Home Nurse; or, Upon Learning That Certain Flowers Feed on Fertilizer Made from Human Remains"

Tupelo Quarterly: "Manifesto with Honey and Bullets"

West Branch: "Creation Myth" ("I wanted to be kissed, not bitten,")

"Shooter" additionally appeared in *Underneath (The University of Canberra Vice-Chancellor's Poetry Prize Anthology)*, 2015.

I owe a further debt of gratitude to the poets whose work has influenced my own. "Insect Life of Michigan" is written after Lynda Hull's poem "Insect Life of Florida." "No matter how many times I pass" is inspired by Tyehimba Jess's "double-jointed" poems from the collections *Leadbelly* and *Olio*. "The Problem with Metamorphosis" borrows its rhetorical structure from Fatimah Asghar's poem "Partition." The first "Creation Myth" begins with a line supplied by C. Dale Young: "I wanted to be kissed, not bitten." The second "Creation Myth" begins with the line "There [is] no more imagination, we [are] in it now," from Joy Harjo's poem "The Book of Myths." "No Thanks" is in conversation with W. S. Merwin's poem "Thanks." "The Cookout" is written after Jason Shinder's poem "The Party."

The path to this book has often felt long. As a result, the list of people to thank is too numerous to count. I've done my best to account for at least a few of those names, below.

Deepest appreciation to Marisa Siegel and the team at Northwestern University Press for believing in this book. It makes a world of difference.

I am forever grateful to the friends and colleagues who read early drafts of these poems over the years, and whose rigor, support, and guidance helped this book find its shape: Fatimah Asghar, Nandi Comer, Vievee Francis, Carlos Andrés Gómez, A. Van Jordan, Jenneva Kayser, J. Estanislao Lopez, Hieu Minh Nguyen, Cynthia Dewi Oka, Matthew Olzmann, and Jayson P. Smith.

Thank you to my instructors at the MFA Program for Writers at Warren Wilson College: Gabrielle Calvocoressi, Daisy Fried, Heather McHugh, and C. Dale Young. And to Deb Allbery for nurturing such a singular space for writers.

This book is in no small way about growing from boyhood into manhood, whatever that may mean. I'm blessed to have a village of friends who have accompanied me along that journey: Dan, Jake, Kevin, Mike, Tom, and Will.

This book is also the product of working across artistic forms and disciplines. Thank you to the friends and colleagues outside poetry who share their work and critiques with equal generosity, and whose influence appears in these poems in myriad ways: Sam Bailey, Scott Beck, Gina Brandolino, Benjamin Dell, Priscila Garcia-Jacquier, Julia Glausi, Connie Huang, Christopher Knauer, Richard Brandon Manus, Bash Naran, Andrés Reconco, Terri Sarris, Idrissa Simmonds-Nastili, Sara Thomason, Bryan Woods, and Michael Zakalik.

Thank you to Jin Auh and the Wylie Agency for your early faith in my work.

Love to members of the Detroit School—some whom I met in the earliest stages of my career, others I'm fortunate to have found along the way—for claiming me despite being (I'll own it) the baby of the group.

Although their names appear elsewhere, they bear repeating: this book would not be possible without the life-changing mentorship—and friendship—of Vievee Francis and A. Van Jordan.

Tender thanks to Mary Anne Lushe for a lifetime of movie nights, long coffees, and good books. Our conversations across time first encouraged, later informed, my ideas about art.

Endless gratitude to and for my parents, Tom Janes and Eleanor Payson. Your example informs every step I take, and your love gives me the courage to chase even the work that scares me most.

Finally, to Tina—I am who I am because of our life together, which means this book is greatly owed to you. Poems here (and poems to come) express more fully my gratitude for your partnership, but for now, for always: I love you. Thank you.